how to have fun with a flower garden

by Editors of Creative
Illustrated by Nancy Inderieden

creative
education
craft series

Published by Creative Education, 123 South Broad Street,
P. O. Box 227, Mankato, Minnesota 56001
Copyright © 1974 by Creative Education. International copyrights reserved in all countries.
No part of this book may be reproduced in any form without written permission
from the publisher. Printed in the United States.
Distributed by Childrens Press, 1224 West Van Buren Street, Chicago, Illinois 60607
Library of Congress Numbers: 74-12442   ISBN: 0-87191-364-X

Library of Congress Cataloging in Publication Data
Creative Education Inc., Mankato, Minn.
How to have fun with a flower garden.
(Creative education craft series)
SUMMARY: Simple instructions for planting and caring for a flower garden.
1. Flower gardening—Juvenile literature. [1. Flower gardening. 2. Gardening]
I. Inderieden, Nancy, illus. II. Title.
SB406.5.C73   1974   635.9   74-12442   ISBN 0-87191-364-X

About Flower Gardens

Our garden flowers have all been developed from wild plants. Ancient civilizations learned that they could use these wild plants by planting them into gardens. The gardens were used as borders around homes and buildings. The early gardens included flowers as well as shrubs, trees, and vines. The temple gardens in ancient Egypt included vegetables, grain, fruit, herbs, and trees along with the flowers.

Gardening advanced rapidly throughout Europe during the Renaissance. Gardens were organized to include flowers, herbs, fruit trees, clipped trees, lawns, and hedges. Fountains, statues, and pools were added to the gardens to make them more attractive. Gardening spread from country to country. Each country tried to develop gardens in special ways. All of these different kinds of gardens were brought to America.

Flower gardens today can be very large and showy or as simple as a small window box of flowers. Many people grow flowers as a hobby. But some people make a living by selling flowers in greenhouses and florist shops.

There are many garden clubs and organizations formed by people who get together to show their flowers and to help others grow gardens.

Almost every country today has a national flower to represent it, and each state in the United States has a state flower. It is fun not only to grow the flowers but also to pick them for decorations or for a special gift for someone else.

Let's Begin

Growing flowers is not hard. It does not take a special talent or a "green thumb." It requires your patience and your care. You must not plant your garden and then forget about it.

Begin by planning your garden. Don't start out by trying to plant a large area or by planting many different kinds of flowers. Begin with a very small garden. Once you are a little better acquainted with the flowers and the care they need, you can add other kinds of flowers.

You must decide first what flower you want to plant. Be sure that you have the right area for the flower before planting it. Almost all garden flowers need a lot of sun. They should be planted in good, rich soil. The best kind of soil for most garden flowers has a lot of clay and humus (humus is vegetable matter that is decaying) and a little sand. Just be sure that the soil in which you will plant your flowers is not dry and sandy. Also, do not plant them on banks, hills, or sloping areas; or the water will drain out of the soil too fast.

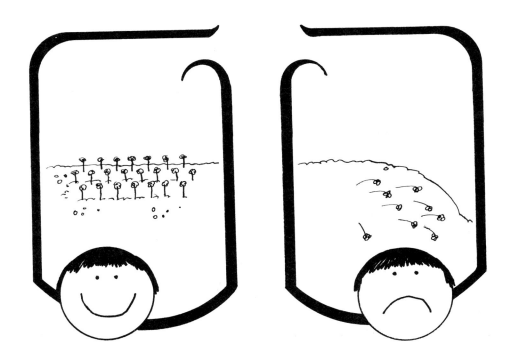

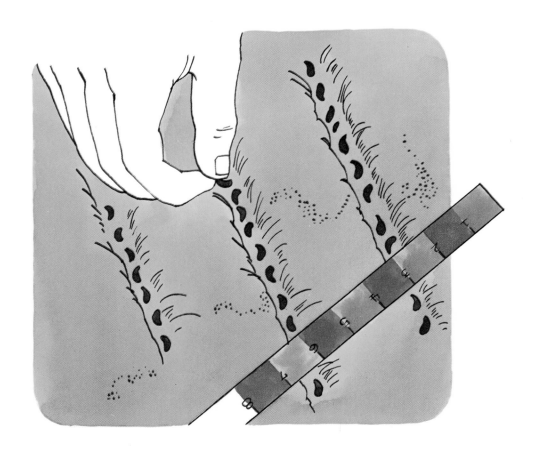

When you begin planting your flowers, check to see that you are planting them as deep as they need to be planted. Most seeds do not need to be planted very deep, but some bulbs must be planted deep. Also, when you are planting seeds, you want to plant enough so that you are sure some will grow.

The three kinds of flowers found in most flower gardens are:

Annuals. These flowers will live for only one year. They must be planted each year.

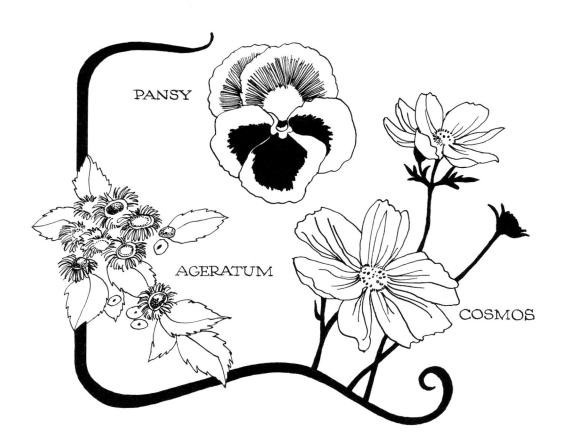

PANSY

AGERATUM

COSMOS

Biennials. These flowers take two years to grow. Usually they do not bloom until the second year. Then they die and must be planted again.

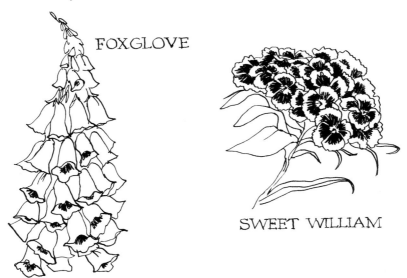

FOXGLOVE

SWEET WILLIAM

Perennials. These flowers live for more than two years. They do not have to be planted yearly as they grow from a stem underground.

Now, we are ready to begin planting some easy flowers.

LILY

Easy Flowers

Here are some popular garden flowers that you can begin with. You should be able to grow any of these flowers without much trouble. Again, start by planting only one or two kinds.

A geranium is a plant that you can grow indoors or outside. They look very nice in the house during the winter months. It will be easiest for you to buy a small geranium plant. You can replant it when you get it home. A geranium does not need rich soil. But be sure that it gets a lot of sun. It should be watered only when the surface of the soil is dry because too much water will kill this plant.

Another easy flower to grow is the sunflower. This is an annual garden flower that does need a lot of sun.

The soil should be quite rich. Since this does grow very tall (6-8 feet), be sure to plant it in back of your other plants. Do not plant these seeds until late spring when the danger of a frost is over. Plant the seeds about ¾-inch deep and at least 3 inches apart. Press the soil down over the seeds. As the first sprouts come up, thin them out to about 6 or 7 inches apart. As they grow taller, thin them out again about 20 inches apart.

Marigolds and zinnias are also easy flowers for your garden. Plant these seeds in regular garden soil. Be sure they will get plenty of sun. You can plant them indoors in the early spring and then transplant the plants outside late in the spring once the danger of a frost is over. Plant the seeds about ⅛-inch deep. Cover, and press the dirt on top of each seed. When the plants are about 2 inches high, thin them out so that they are about 4 inches apart. They will bloom near the end of summer and into fall.

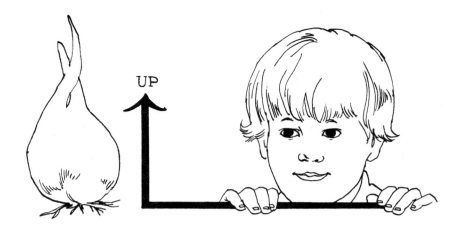

The tulip grows from a bulb rather than a seed. Tulip bulbs are planted in the fall. Be sure to put the bulb in the ground the correct way — pointed end up. Bulbs should be planted about 4 to 5 inches deep in average soil. Put them at least 4 inches apart.

Another flower that grows from a bulb is the daffodil. This bulb is planted in the fall. Bulbs should be planted about 4 inches deep and 5 inches apart. Again make sure the right end of the bulb is up. These pretty yellow flowers bloom in the early spring.

The iris also grows from a bulb. It can be planted in the fall or early in the spring in average soil. The bulbs should be planted about 3 inches deep. The iris blooms about midsummer.

Gladioli also grow from bulbs. These should be planted early in the spring, but one must be careful of a late frost. Gladioli grow best in rich, soft soil and need lots of water and sun. Plant the bulbs about 4 inches deep. In the fall after the gladioli have bloomed, you must dig up the gladioli bulbs and keep them indoors during the winter. Then they can again be planted in the spring.

Care of Your Flower Garden

Once you have planted your seeds or bulbs, the care begins. Here are a few ways to help you become a good flower gardener.

If you are planting bulbs in the fall to bloom in the early spring, you will want to cover them after they have been planted. Put leaves and grass cuttings on top of the soil where your bulbs are.

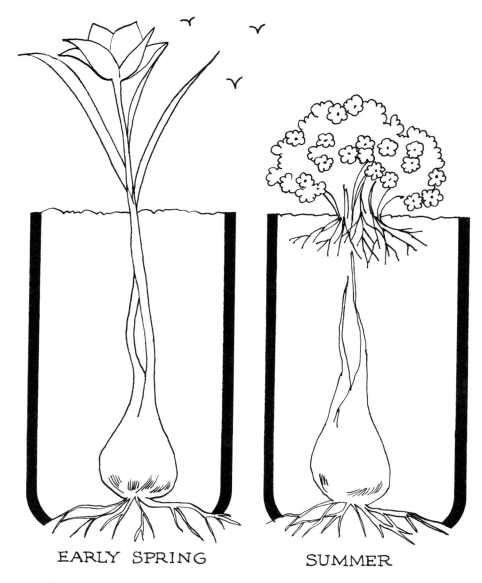

EARLY SPRING   SUMMER

In the spring when you are planting other
flowers in the garden, be sure that you do not dig
up the bulbs. Once the early spring blooming flowers
have died, you can plant annuals in the soil on top
of the bulbs without removing the bulbs.

After the flowers are planted, you must be sure to water the soil whenever necessary. When it is necessary for you to water your flowers, do not sprinkle them. It is best to use a hose to soak the soil thoroughly. It will also help to keep the moisture in the soil longer if you put leaves, weeds that have been pulled, and grass cuttings around the stems. The best time of the day to water your flowers is the evening.

Be sure to remove weeds as soon as they appear in your garden. They will keep your flowers from growing properly if allowed to stay. You can either pull the weeds or dig them out. Be careful, if you dig them up, not to dig up the roots of your flowers.

If you have planted your seeds very close, weed out those that are not very strong. This will allow the strong ones a better chance to grow.

28

Picking the flowers will help your plants to keep blooming.

When your flowers quit blooming, they should be removed from the soil.

In the fall is the best time to prepare your soil for a spring garden. Plant the bulbs which bloom in early spring. The rest of the garden should then be prepared by using a hoe to break up the soil. Do not rake the garden. Let it freeze this way. Then in the spring when you are ready to plant, rake the garden. Make sure that it is level before you plant.

The real fun in having a garden comes when your flowers are in bloom. Pick your flowers often. This helps them to keep blooming. Be sure to share your flowers with others. You can even learn how to dry your flowers for a nice winter bouquet!

how to have fun

BAKING COOKIES AND CAKES
BUILDING SAILBOATS
KNITTING
WITH MACRAME
MAKING BIRDHOUSES AND FEEDERS
MAKING BREAKFAST
MAKING CHRISTMAS DECORATIONS
MAKING KITES
MAKING MOBILES
MAKING PAPER AIRPLANES
MAKING PUPPETS
WITH NEEDLEPOINT
SEWING
WEAVING
WITH AN INDOOR GARDEN
MAKING RUGS
MAKING LUNCH
MAKING DINNER
WITH A VEGETABLE GARDEN
WITH A FLOWER GARDEN
MAKING EASTER DECORATIONS
MAKING HOLIDAY DECORATIONS
MAKING GREETING CARDS
PRESSING FLOWERS
WITH DECOUPAGE

**creative
education
craft series**

91

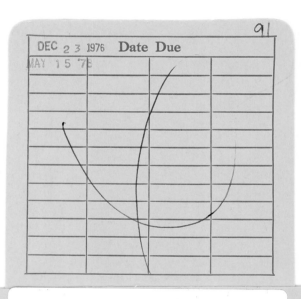

DEC 2 3 1976 **Date Due**

MAY 1 5 78